"WHAT WILL HAPPEN TO ME?"

Every night, approximately three million children go to bed with a parent in prison or jail. Here are their thoughts and stories.

by HOWARD ZEHR and LORRAINE STUTZMAN AMSTUTZ
portraits by HOWARD ZEHR

Good Books

Intercourse, PA 17534
800/762-7171
www.GoodBooks.com

ACKNOWLEDGMENTS

We are grateful to Nell Bernstein for her pioneering work with children whose parents are incarcerated and for graciously allowing us to include a quote from her landmark work, *All Alone in the World: Children of the Incarcerated*, by Nell Bernstein, published by The New Press, New York, New York, 2005.

"A Set of Core Principles for Policy Development" is used by permission of Dee Ann Newell. We are grateful to Dee Ann for her enthusiastic support and guidance in this project.

"Children of Incarcerated Parents: A Bill of Rights" is the work of the San Francisco Children of Incarcerated Parents Partnership (www.sfcipp.org), which is supported by the Zellerbach Family Foundation.

Design by Cliff Snyder

Library of Congress Cataloging-in-Publication Data
Zehr, Howard.
    What will happen to me? / by Howard Zehr and Lorraine Stutzman Amstutz ; portraits by Howard Zehr.
        p. cm.
    "Every night, approximately three million children go to bed with a parent in prison or jail. Here are their thoughts and stories."
    ISBN 978-1-56148-689-2 (pbk. : alk. paper) 1. Children of prisoners–United States. 2. Children of prisoners–Services for–United States. 3. Prisoners' families–United States. I. Amstutz, Lorraine Stutzman. II. Title.
    HV8886.U5Z44 2011
    362.82'95092273–dc22   2010012419

TABLE OF CONTENTS

A Few Words to Begin   2

PART I: **The Children**   5

PART II: **For Caregivers**   53
    Ten Questions Often Asked by Children Whose
        Parents Are in Prison   60
    Dealing with Emotions   65
    Staying in Touch   69
    Finding Moments of Celebration   71
    When a Parent Returns   72
    Self-Care for Family Caregivers   74
    Suggestions for Third-Party Caregivers   76
    "It Makes You Stronger"   78

PART III: **A Matter of Justice**   79
    Children of Incarcerated Parents: A Bill of Rights   83
    A Matter of Justice   84

Appendix
    A: Bill of Rights for Children of the Incarcerated and
        Some Policy Implications   89
    B: A Set of Core Principles for Policy Development   91

Suggested Resources   92
Endnotes   93
About the Authors and Photographer   94

A FEW WORDS TO BEGIN

My mom is somewhere—I don't know where—but she isn't here with me. It can't be good because it seems like a big secret. Grandma says she's away getting an education, that she loves me, that she'll be back when she's learned her lessons. What lessons? Why can't she learn them here, with me?

My teacher looks at me funny when the subject of parents comes up. The other kids whisper and say nasty things: "Your mother was bad. She's a crook."

When it's parents' day at school, the other kids bring their mom and dads. I bring Nana. She's a lot older than the other adults.

I know other kids who are missing a parent, some of them both parents, but I feel something shameful about my mom. I'm just not sure what it is.

I worry about her. I wonder whether I'm like her. If she's done something bad, does that mean I'll follow in her footsteps? Did she leave because I did something bad?

I think about her a lot. I dream about her. What is she like? Is she safe? Do I really have a mother? Does she love me? Why isn't she here, taking care of me?

I feel alone. Sometimes I think I'm the only kid like this.

In fact, there are at least three million other children in America in similar situations.

This book is about and, in a sense by, children who have one or both parents in prison. Some of the issues they name are faced by all children who have absent parents. But, there are special challenges and pains when a parent is in prison.

What Will Happen to Me? is also about, and for, those who are caregivers of such children—thousands of grandparents who are raising these children, millions of teachers, school counselors, and social workers who interact with them daily.

Through the voices of these families come the challenges and hardships they face, but also the remarkable resilience and spirit they often demonstrate. Based on their experiences, the book suggests themes and strategies that may be helpful to caregivers and perhaps to the children, too.

ABOUT THIS BOOK

We have organized the book into three sections. The majority of the book, PART I, includes the faces and voices of children. PART II is especially for caregivers. It includes a few portraits and voices of grandparents, as well as some suggestions for understanding and responding to the needs of these children. PART III considers the justice issues raised by these families' situations.

We began this project because we wanted to give voice and visibility to these often-forgotten children who are so profoundly affected by circumstances and policies that do not take their needs into account. We interviewed and did photographic portraits of children of various ages in a number of communities across the country. From that material, we created an exhibit that is now available on loan through the Mennonite Central Committee Audiovisual Library. (See *Suggested Resources*, page 92, for more information.)

As we got further into the project, we became more and more aware of the burden put on caregivers, especially family members and often grandparents, who take care of children whose parents are incarcerated.

The young people featured here are predominately children of color. While their numbers may be somewhat over-represented in this book when compared to the number of persons of color in the U.S., their presence generally reflects proportionately the overall reality of the prison population in this country. We believe that people of color are over-represented in prison primarily because of law enforcement and sentencing policies that impact communities of color most heavily. However, the impact of parental incarceration on children, no matter their race or cultural background, is profound, and many of the issues they face are universal.

OUR INTEREST IN THIS SUBJECT

The two of us who have undertaken this project have been colleagues in the field of restorative justice for many years, working with those who have offended, those who have been offended against, and their families. Howard has done several photo/interview books that present the voices and photos of victims and their families, and of life-sentenced prisoners (See *Suggested Resources*, page 92). Lorraine's thesis (for the Masters in Social Work degree) focused on children with parents in prison.

OUR GRATITUDE

So many individuals and organizations have contributed to this project that it is hard to know where to begin and end. For financial support, we acknowledge the Annie E. Casey Foundation, the Fransen Foundation, the Victim Offender Mediation Association, and Joseph and Barbara Gascho. For financial support that helped make time to work on this project possible, we thank John and Kathyrn Fairfield and Ruth and Tim Jost. Individuals who contributed knowledge and connections include Jacqueline Shock, Nariman Elias, Michael Bischoff, Teya Sepinuck, and Erica Fricke. Organizations that collaborated or assisted in some way are The Center for Justice and Peacebuilding at Eastern Mennonite University, the Mennonite Central Committee U.S. Office on Peace and Justice, Arkansas Voices for the Children Left Behind, TOVA: Artistic Projects for Social Change, and the Council on Crime and Justice (Minneapolis).

We especially thank Dee Ann Newell for her enthusiastic support and advice throughout this project and for her indispensable assistance in developing strategies to reach the intended audiences.

Photographic projects with children are always challenging because of the confidentiality and permission issues they raise. We deeply appreciate the program staff and the parents and guardians who understood the value of this project and were willing to have their clients and loved ones participate.

Above all, we want to thank those young people and grandparents who so generously lent their voices.

HOWARD ZEHR
LORRAINE STUTZMAN AMSTUTZ

PART I

The Children

"These children have committed no crime, but the price they are forced to pay is steep. They forfeit, too, much of what matters to them: their homes, their safety, their public status and private self-image, their primary source of comfort and affection. Their lives are profoundly affected..."

—Nell Bernstein, *All Alone in the World*

NYVEAH WITH PRESTON

Can I give Daddy a hug? I wanna give Daddy a hug!

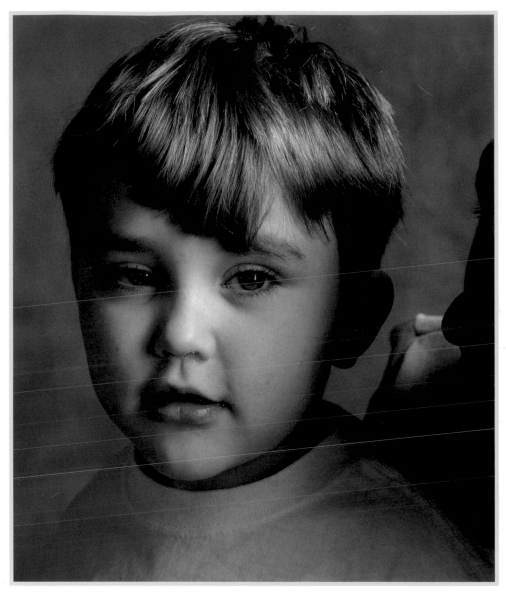

JACOB

JACOB: Mommy, remember when you was in jail? I was really, really sad. Sad that you didn't come home. I love you.

LISA, JACOB'S MOTHER: I'm very lucky and fortunate. I mean, this kid loves me! He won't let me out of his sight. He says, "Mama, why did you go to jail?" I say, "I wasn't being good, Jacob; that's what happens."

We didn't even know why she left. They just came and got her. My grandma came to school and got us. She didn't explain nothing. My dad went into prison not too much after that. That's my stepdad. And then my auntie went in. They all went in on the same charges.

It was hard for me because I had to change schools. I had to make new friends. It was very hard, and then my family was dying, and it was hard on me 'cause I couldn't go to their funerals. They had no way to get us up there.

It was really hard. Everybody else, they got their moms and their dads. My mom wasn't with me, to be there for my games and stuff, to watch me. She *was* there before when she was out; she was there for me all the time. Most of my friends, they didn't understand it, they were like, "What's going on?" It's something I really don't talk about.

Visiting was hard 'cause you know you're leaving and your mom's not leaving with you.

Now that my mom's out we can do things. She can be there for me, she can take me places, get clothes, you know, do what moms do. Now I can go see my family, visit and go to family reunions, go to my family funerals when they die.

AMNESSIA

AMNESSIA

My father was locked up 15 years. I asked my mom and stepdad about it. The answers I got said it was something serious, but they weren't going to tell me about it. I waited for them to say something, but they never did. To this day I fear that it could happen to me. If what happened to him happens to me, will I react the same way and put myself in the same position?

Growing up was kinda lonely. My father wrote me letters, but I just skimmed them. It was like he was a stranger—like, who is this guy, sending these letters? I knew he was my dad, but.... If I had known the truth, it probably would've made me more interested in reading the letters.

Having my father in prison changed my life by causing me to be by myself more. And it made me get involved; I try to do things for other people rather than myself. It's almost like A.D.D. I have to do something, I have to try to achieve more.

Why am I doing this all? You feel like there's a deeper problem or issue that you gotta solve, but you can't figure out what it is. It's hard to get at the roots of it. Maybe one day I'll find out the meaning of all this, why he got locked up and stuff like that. One day it's gonna unravel and I'll find out why. And hopefully make my life better.

JERMAINE

JERMAINE

TIEANA

My dad was gone for about three years. They said he was in college. Every time he was gone he always talked to me and wrote me letters and everything. He's a good artist, and every time he wrote me a letter, he drew something in it. One time he drew me a mermaid, and it was really good.

I miss my mom, and I don't know where she is. I just worry 'cause something might happen to her, and I will never know because she doesn't call or anything.

I like living with my grandparents. They spoil me. They give me things like a piano. I've been playing since second grade. I'm happy.

JALON

My grandma filled in for my mom until she came back. So she was kind of acting like my mom. When my mom was gone, I'd cry myself to sleep.

I don't really know my dad. He's still alive but, I wonder, is he getting hurt in jail or something like that? I want him back so I can be with him.

I want them around so we could have a family.

JASMINE

I felt so sad. I was just crying. It just made my head hurt, my brain hurt, my stomach hurt. It just got control of me. It got my mind twisted. I couldn't focus on anything else....

A whole lot of days I couldn't go to sleep without my mom. I had some bad dreams, so my daddy gave me an invisible necklace.

It helped me dream about my mom. I had a dream that she had come back. I was walking, I opened my eyes and saw my mom, and I grabbed her.

I couldn't live without her. It was like a curse. It was like a prison. I'm just glad she's back now.

SHAUN

I didn't go along to visit last time. I wanted to play with my friends that day. I was a little bit angry 'cause she's been there so many times. I want her to get out.

I was three when he got locked up. I have some memories—we were at the circus and we were riding on an elephant. It had to be a dream.

When he was in prison I had this grudge against him for not being here for me. When I finally got a chance to talk to him, and he let me know what really happened, I'm like, "Oh, I didn't know that." I had jumped to so many conclusions. I had a newfound respect for him, and I realized he really did love me.

Sometimes now I dream about a situation that has happened to me. I know he wasn't there, but he'll be there this time. He'll be talking to me, like my conscience. He'll talk me through it. He'll be the person that takes the mask off everything and tells me how it really is. **SASHA**

Sasha's father was on death row. His conviction was overturned and he was released, but he died five years later of untreated hepatitis.

SASHA

When I first went down to the prison, it was real hard being able to hug my mama and touch her and then not take her with me. It was hard. We all cried, but now I'm just used to it. But I miss my mama and I need her.

I really had to be the mama for my sisters. I wanted things to be right for them. My aunt says I've never really been able to be a child. Now that I'm 18, it's just like I'm 21 or something. It's like I'm still older than I really am. Now my aunt says I should be able to have a little bit of that childhood that I never got to have back then.

I used to be ashamed to say my mom is in prison. But then my auntie told me that it's not my fault. So it's nothing I should be ashamed of. It's nothing I did.

I do have a friend—she goes to the same school—and her mama and my mama are down there together. I can talk to her 'cause she knows how I'm feeling inside. She's been there.

I'll probably have kids by the time she gets out. Taking them to the jailhouse—that's not where I want them to remember her from.

I just want people to be proud of me. That's why I keep going. I'm a very cheerful person. They say at school that I just brighten up people's day.

DEEDEE

DEEDEE

LATRELL

I don't really talk about it.

Latrell's father, whom he never met and only spoke to once on the phone, is in prison. His stepfather has been in and out of prison, and his mother, who was also in prison, died recently of a drug overdose. He lives with his grandmother.

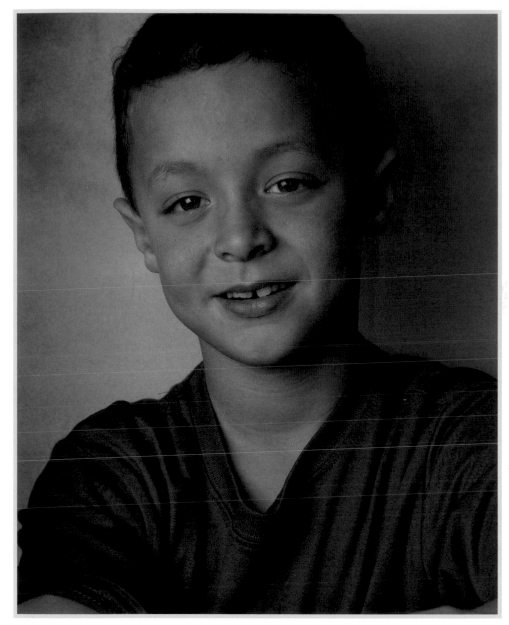

TYLER

I like to visit my mother. I write to her sometimes. I keep the letters. She draws pictures and Grandma keeps them for me.
I'd rather not talk to others at school about it.

I was three when my mom went in. And then my dad went in and my mama got out. And then she went back in.

Life would've been different if my parents hadn't been in prison. I would have been graduating high school this year, going to senior prom, and doing all the other stuff kids do instead of growing up too fast.

I had to grow up real quick. I've lived on the streets, I've lived with friends, family, boyfriends. I've done it all. I'm fixing to be 18, and I never thought I'd make it to see 16.

Because I wasn't in school, I had no education. I was living on my own on the streets and I thought that somebody would kill me. I thought I'd be dead. But I'm still standing. I'm cheerful. What I've been through has made me who I am today. I'm not a weak-minded person. I'm very strong.

I like church. Sometimes I feel God is talking directly to me. Any church I go to, they say things that relate to me. So I am like, "Dang, is He talking to me?"

If you have a mom or dad locked up, it's not your fault. It's nobody's fault but theirs; they made their choices. They decided to go down that road, not you. Don't feel guilty for their mistakes.

BRITTANY

BRITTANY

My father started getting arrested when I was around five.

And my brother is in prison.

I was always pressured to keep things together, 'cause everything was so chaotic. I just wanted to be free of problems. I thought if I moved as far away as possible, I wouldn't have to deal with anything. But being far away didn't stop the fact that I still have to deal with everything, even though I wasn't physically there anymore.

It was something you weren't supposed to talk about outside the house. Once I got older, I found friends I trusted and actually talked about it. But sometimes you wonder how much good it really is to talk about it. My friends can sympathize, but they don't really know what it is like.

I'm trying to find some way to express everything I'm feeling through my artwork. But I'm not sure if I'm comfortable with explaining it, especially with a bunch of strangers in my college class.

When I watch my baby, it's inspiring. My son is the best thing that could have happened to me. Family is central. Even though it often didn't work, sometimes it does.

ANABEL

ANABEL

I remember when they came and got her. I was sad, I really was. I was crying because it was hard to see them come and take my mom. I was mad at everybody. You could say I was mad at the world. I didn't want to talk to nobody, to tell people how I felt, didn't want to be around nobody. I took my anger out on other people.

At times it's like I'm mad at her for not being here, for being locked up. You know, she shouldn't have done what she did. But then again at times I feel sad, 'cause she's there and she's not here with me. I just can't have her around like I want.

I felt like nobody could understand what I was going through 'cause they probably didn't have it happen to them. So didn't nobody understand me. You know, I was just misunderstood.

I do have one friend who understands. I can talk to her about it; I know that she understands, you know, because one of her parents is in prison. Sometimes that helps. It's better for me to let it out. I don't have to carry around all that weight anymore—it is better to talk about it.

At church I praise-dance and I wish my mom could be there to see that. And just last Wednesday at my school we had a Black History play and I was in that. I wish she could've seen that. And the pageant that's coming up—wish she was here to see me do that.

I want other kids to know that even though your parents are locked up, they're not bad people. They just did something that they shouldn't have done. And it really affects us, the kids. It really does. And I want them to know that we'll get through it. As long as we have someone that's there to help us, we can get through it. It makes you stronger—I know it's made me stronger. You have to grow up fast.

TAYLOR

TAYLOR

TREYVON

Sometimes I go to see my mom on weekends, and sometimes when I get out of school and sometimes after church. When I see her I'm real happy. And when I have to leave, I'm sad. I wanna be all together.

ANDREW

I was 9 when he went in. Now I'm 11. It makes me kind of angry and sad. It's hard that I really don't get to spend any time with him. I wish he could get his life straightened out.

My mom's been in and out of prison since I was like two or three. I have dreams, many dreams: we are all living under one roof, my dad, my mom, my little sister, me and my brother, and my other little sister. All of us in one house. We all have our own rooms. I used to love those dreams. Now I just have dreams about my mom dying.

I feel real comfortable talking to my friend Cassandra 'cause she's going through the same thing I'm going through. And the program with Mr. Ted from SKIP (Support for Kids with Incarcerated Parents) has been real helpful. I never used to open up until he came to the school. I felt like I had somebody listening to me, somebody to talk to. Now I know that I'm not the only one who has a problem—there's other people in the world that have the same problems.

ERIN

ERIN

I don't know why he's in there. I heard so many different stories. So I just wait until I find out the truth.

I don't want no part of him because he wasn't even around when I was growing. I don't want to see no letters or anything. It was his loss all these years. When he gets out, I don't need him to be coming in, messing up what I have. I'll just focus on school. I'd rather stay on track. I don't think of him— I'm in my own world.

My friend, the way I can relate to her is that her father died. I know how it feels to have a loss.

My grandma tells me, and a lot of my teachers, everybody says, "You're very mature for your age." At first I didn't even know what it means. I used to be like, What is mature? Is that a bad thing or a good thing? But now I know.

SHANIKA

SHANIKA

BRITTANIE

I hated my mom when she first went in. I thought she didn't love us. But I also missed her. I'd feel mad, and then I'd just start crying because I knew she wanted to be with us, that she did love us. People would tell me that she wasn't in there because she didn't love us. She was in there because she made a mistake, and she did want to get out and be with us.

I had one friend I would talk to about it. Sometimes everyone tries to make it sound like it was some nice experience, when it is just bad.

If this does happen to someone, I tell them to talk to people instead of keeping it in 'cause that just makes it worse. And they love you and they didn't do it to hurt you. They just made some mistakes.

JASMINE

My dad's kind of on and off going to prison. I kinda don't want him to be a dad to me because of all the things he's done. But if he changed, I would love for him to be a dad to me. I would like to be able to talk to somebody besides my mom. That'd be nice, somebody having another opinion about my life.

JESSIE

My stepdad writes me a lot. I write back, and I write my brother back, too. My brother is getting out, though, in like two months. I tell them we're gonna play war. It's like paintball, but there are little bitty plastic BBs. Play in the backyard, out in the woods. I wanna go out in the woods.

LYNISA

When I visited my mom, I talked, and I used to take pictures
with her. In my dreams I thought she was coming back. And I was
happy when she did come back.

*D*ear Dad. I hope you're doing fine. I prayed for you and I'm going to pray for you tonight. I hope you won't have to have any surgery. I really don't want you to have any surgeries because they hurt. I hope you get your favorite kind of medicine you need to take, a flavor that you like.

I went to culture night again, and this time I didn't drum. I want to wait until you come home to drum with you because you're my favorite dad and the best dad I could have.

I think you're the greatest drum teacher for me. I know one dance move already. And you can teach me some dance moves for the drum.

I hope you have a good week. I love you, Dad.

TRAVIS

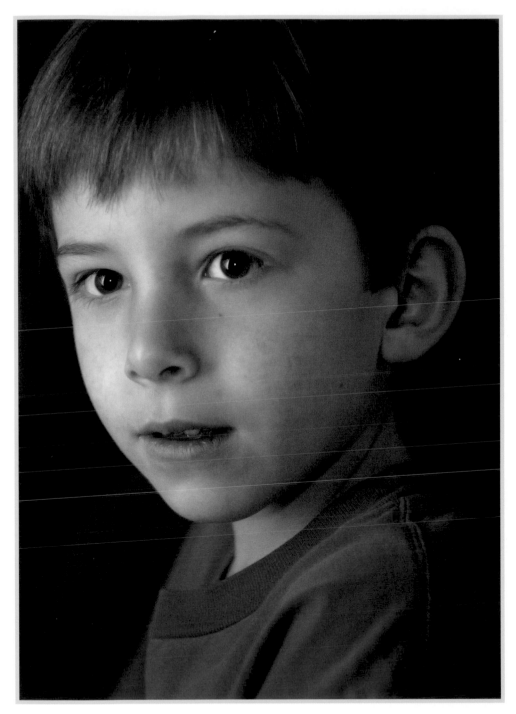

TRAVIS

Visits with my dad are fine. I can get to touch him…well, I did get to touch him sometimes, and it is so much fun because they have pizza, nachos, anything that you could eat.

Sometimes he just starts talking a lot and getting up on where his life is, and then I start getting up on how my life is. He asks me lots of questions. I ask him questions, and we write each other.

When I was little I used to be scared, and people were always trying to talk about it. Some of their parents are not in jail. They just have an easy life. My life is kinda horrible, kinda bad.

There's so much to do with him that I haven't even done yet. I haven't had Christmas with him…I haven't had Valentine's with him…haven't done nothing. Haven't had New Years with him. Nothin'.

I pray for him every night so God can let him get out for one year. Like it ain't over yet, 'cause last year I told God to let him get out for one year. But all I know is it's not over yet 'cause this year's not over.

PATRICK

PATRICK

I missed a lot. Like last year at my school there was a father-daughter dance. My friends asked me what I was wearing, and I said I wasn't going. I had bought the dress—I don't know why. I was looking at the dress, imagining just me and my dad. I started crying. That's what makes me miss my father the most.

Sometimes when I'm alone, I sit there and look up and close my eyes and think, "If he were here, what would happen?" I would have had my full life. It's just half now. I'm starting not to care about it. He's there, I'm over here, and I'm gonna do what I'm gonna do.

My sweet 16 birthday, I've been planning and planning it. I want a circle with me coming out with my partner, and then he hands me over to my dad. Then it hits me, my dad isn't gonna be there. It has to be my grandfather. It's gonna be that way. I might as well get used to it.

CASSANDRA

CASSANDRA

MARANDA

I would be thinking about my mom before I went to sleep. I had a counselor, but I didn't talk to her. I just talked to her about problems with my friends 'cause I don't like spreading that around about my mom. It makes me sad.

It felt good when my mom came back. And when my dad comes back, I want to take him out to eat and go swimming and do other things. Go to the movies.

KEVIN

If my stepmom were here, we would see her every day, and it would be happy and everything.

She missed my honors assembly. Missed a lot of parent-teacher conferences—some parent things where they go to the school and talk to them about how good or bad we've been in school.

When she comes home it's gonna be good, 'cause now she's Christian. I hope all the stuff she's saying, she gonna do. I hope it stays like that. People ask, When you are 21, will you still stay with your mom? I will, 'cause I'm gonna try to make up all the time. So I hope when she gets home, she do good.

If she got out I would be so happy. I would just die, breaking out crying. They'd be tears of joy, though. I'd be so happy to see my mom come home. I miss her. I go to school, make my good grades, and I'm gonna try to graduate next year so when she come home, she can have something. I want her to be able to have stuff. When she got incarcerated, we lost everything.

I would tell other kids to take every moment to enjoy your parents because once your mama's gone, there's nothing you can do about it.

LA'CHASTA

LA'CHASTA

Someone in my family told me once that my father got arrested the night I was born. He went in and out for minor offenses after that and spent five years in a federal prison in North Carolina. He was an alcoholic and was very, very violent. I would see him intermittently from about the time I was 13 until he passed away. I was 25 when he died.

I wasn't told for a long time that he was in prison. I found out through my cousin. We were playing one day at a family gathering, and they decided to let me in on the big secret. I was crushed. I felt so betrayed, by my mother especially. And I was embarrassed that I did not know. They had this piece of knowledge that I should have had. Although I always knew something wasn't right. I was told, "Daddy is in North Carolina working and going to school." I was thinking, "That's odd."

His family didn't want me to know because they didn't want me to think poorly of him. My mother didn't tell me because she didn't want to upset me, to have me carry that burden. I don't know if I could have articulated it at that time, but I was aware that things weren't right.

As I got older I didn't know who I could trust to tell. There were a few teachers I could invite in, and that turned out to be a really good experience. And there were a few friends I could invite in. But their parents... that wasn't a good idea. So it was hard to navigate. But I definitely needed to know.

I remember the first weekend he came back after I knew. I was in third grade. I stayed with him and my grandmother. I wasn't very close to her. She was stressed out when he would come home, and so it was awkward. My grandfather was an alcoholic and abusive, and then she saw my dad coming back and she had to be responsible for him, too, and then me. And she had to take care of her dying mother, so it was too much.

When he left, when my mother and father split up, I had this feeling that if I am good enough, he'll come back. I just really wanted him to come back. If I did something wrong, my mom would say, "If you don't stop, I am gonna tell your father, and he is not going to want to see you anymore." I remember that just scared me to death. I wanted to see him very badly.

It was in therapy years later that I tried to name that feeling. "Longing" was what I came up with. It was something that was always there. I remember this one day when he was out, I ran up to him and he picked me up and I remember the smell of his shirt

STACEY BOUCHET, PH.D.

and the feeling of my hand on his hair and the back of his neck—that feeling of being held, and how good it felt. But it was the idea of a father that I was longing for, because he never fit the bill.

I would see him periodically over the years as I got older, but it was very awkward. It was never like what I envisioned or wanted it to be. The meetings were kind of painful. It was just this connection that I really wanted, but I don't think he knew how to do it. Nobody knew how to do it. They stuck us together. My grandmother would say, "Take her shopping." It felt awkward and contrived.

I was very, very angry. I had to do a lot of work—letters I never sent—and after he died, I remember I went into a really serious stage of depression. There was a point when I just didn't get up and go to work. When he died, I had to identify the body. I remember I said that I wanted his wallet. They gave it to me, and it had a picture of me when I was in junior high. I kept it and would look at it sometimes.

I had to fight the demons and it took years. I had tried to deal with it earlier. I remember in the fifth grade I had a really wonderful caring teacher, and again in sixth grade. They had me journaling and things like that, really beyond the call of duty. One teacher would let me come almost every day after school and feed me dinner and stuff.

I had different points in my life when I tried to address it. But there were so many periods in my life when it was staring me in the face: "I want my dad, I want a dad, I want a damn dad!" Looking back, it was very evident in my behavior. Like my girlfriends' dads—I attached to them very quickly. And I was acting out a lot.

On the one hand, I felt angry and mad that he was not there, disappointed every time I saw him, because I was not getting what I wanted. On the other hand, I was dying to be with him, to see him, to be a part of him. I remember the feeling was like I just wanted to melt into his body and have him carry me around. I wanted to say, "Just put me in your pocket." I just wanted to be enveloped. Oh my God, it was so strong, that feeling of wanting to be cared for, taken care of, but nothing ever seemed stable and there was no place that I fit.

There was never any place in my family that felt particularly safe. I loved my mother, but I also felt very much like a burden. I always felt like I was the parent. As I got older, I wanted to learn how to set boundaries and how to keep boundaries with people. It was really hard.

At school I felt like I didn't quite fit. I was

different. We were poor, I had a dad who was in prison, my family was really screwed up. I was like a puzzle piece that didn't quite fit.

I think I felt self-imposed stigma. My friends never did anything to make me feel I was less than them, but I always felt like I was less than them. I never ever met another child who said they had a parent incarcerated.

Stigma is huge, and so is loss of control. There is a potential to have a relationship or for good things to happen, but it's taken totally out of your control because of the incarceration.

I was headed down a really bad road. I gained weight, I drank a lot, I was a party and social drinker. I always thought I was different from my father because I never got angry or mean or abusive. I was a fun drunk, the life of a party. But when I got depressed after my father passed away, I started seeing a psychologist. The psychologist said, "I can't say that you are an alcoholic. But I can tell you unequivocally, with your family history you are playing with fire."

My father has five brothers and sisters, and four of them were alcoholics and drug-addicted, too. And my mother is an alcoholic, and her brother, and there is a history of suicide, too. That kind of scared me, but

I was still very self-destructive. Drinking, and a lot of sexual behaviors. At a really young age, my desire to attach to men really opened me to a lot of abusive situations.

What changed? Maybe it was the therapy. I remember my therapist said I should study social work. I had never really thought of myself as intelligent, but she said I was. I had thought about going to college, but I was afraid when I looked at those books. She said, "College is like taking a trip. If you could see the whole road laid out in front of you, you wouldn't ever start. But you can always go just as far as your headlights will show you. Three feet ahead, that's what you concentrate on, and before you know it, you're there."

She talked me into applying for college. And my adviser there basically said the same thing: "You can do it every step of the way." I had three or four professors who believed in me. It took some people believing in me so I could believe in myself. That's when it really started to shift for me. I still struggle with believing in myself even though people say, "You are so outgoing, so self-assured."

I got pregnant while in college. I was a sophomore and they got concerned. My mom said, "Drop out, the baby needs you." But my adviser said, "Don't drop out. I'd like to see what we can do." And I ended that year with a 3.92 and walked across the stage to get an award with my daughter in my arms.

And the same scenario happened again. A professor asked to see me after a session and asked, "Why aren't you getting your Ph.D.? Come to my office tomorrow and you can get the application. And I want you to work for me." And I did.

Going to college changed my life. It was like the blinders came off and I saw a new world coming. No one in my family had ever gone to college. There is a kind of integrity that I learned from college that I never got growing up.

I heard about healing and reconciling with a parent, and I think that would have been valuable for me to experience. I didn't get that chance. I did feel like there were good things about my dad. People would tell me, "You look like your father." I have my dad's eyes, and I love my eyes, my dad's eyes.

I remember my dad wrote me two letters the whole time he was incarcerated. I read those letters over and over. He drew a little Snoopy on one. The thought that he was thinking about me while he was in prison—I can't even say how much it meant to me. It was that connection I was looking for. I was prevented from that by my family

and by the circumstances—he was incarcerated far away in North Carolina.

There is a sense of loss with these experiences, and it should be dealt with in some way. You don't have to beat it to death, but it should be addressed in some sort of therapeutic way. And I think it would have been nice to connect with others who were dealing with the same issues, or even close to the same—even just an absent dad. That would have been nice.

I didn't have formal mentors, but the people who came into my life acted as mentors. They were there for the long haul, and they weren't expecting me to be perfect. I've talked to some adults who as children of incarcerated parents had mentors who, when things got rough—for example, the kids acting out—the mentors left. I think that's the worst thing that can happen. But if mentors continue for at least a year, I think they can make a huge difference.

I think the incarceration of a parent should be a signal to communities and systems that there are things going on in families.

STACEY BOUCHET, PH.D.

PART II

For Caregivers

We're going with the flow. It takes a lot of prayin'. And I try to not get upset with them where I would say the wrong thing that I'll be sorry for. But they're crazy about us!

I remember when Darnell and I used to get in the car on Saturday mornings and go to the market and just mess around all day. It wasn't that much we were doing, but then we had to stop it. It seemed like a lot to us. We just missed our freedom.

Foster parents get money to keep these kids. We can't get nothin,' and we're on a fixed income. There's a lot of things you would like to do that you can't do for that reason. And then when they go gettin' older they think, "Well, why can't I have this somebody else got, and why can't I do that??" There should be more, somehow.

We'd rather raise them up than throw 'em out there and let somebody just half-way kill them or ruin them before they live. We can do what we can do. And we'll feel satisfied.

CAROLYN AND DARNELL HOBBS

CAROLYN AND DARNELL HOBBS AND GRANDCHILDREN

Shaun is 13; I got him at five months. Tyler's eight and I've had him since he was two days old. They are my great-grandchildren.

They play baseball in the summertime. And we have a busy church. Every program they have at church, I keep'm there. I'm in the ballfield every day through the week. Both of them have Big Brothers. Shaun's Big Brother was here yesterday. They went bike-riding and rode about seven or eight miles. Tyler's Big Brother will be here next Friday.

I try to make Christmas as special as I can. I save money and give them one big Christmas present. This year the church brought the boys gifts from their mother.

We always make a big production out of the Christmas tree. Easter is a big thing, too. We do cookies, and we do colored eggs, and we decorate trees out in the yard.

I took Tyler to see his mother before Christmas. He had a good time with her. Shaun wouldn't go see her. He says if his mother really loved him, she wouldn't be where she is. And I wouldn't have to be a mother and daddy.

But I haven't been back to the boys' mother since before Christmas. She's just bugging me for money all the time. You know, it's hard to support these boys and send her money, too. In the last letter, I sent her $20 and I said, "I'm not going to take away from your boys just for you to have potato chips and drinks and these special substances that you think you need."

I used to go out with my friends and eat, but I don't have those friends anymore. One of my best friends has her little granddaughter. She moved and I miss her so much.

I asked for the same thing for Christmas and for my birthday from my family: for two hours on top of Spruce Knob by myself. I didn't get it. That's all I ask for. If they would just take the boys so I can go out on the mountain for two hours by myself, that's all I ask for. But I didn't get it.

To other caregivers I'd say, you need to really think about how far you can go and not crack.

MARTHA AREY

MARTHA AREY

My daughter has been in and out, in and out of prison. Her oldest girl I've kept the majority of her life. I've just been basically raising her kids off and on. Tiana, the nine-year-old, says that her mom makes wrong choices. She's so smart—she's so perfect it scares me. The four-year-old was having imaginary illnesses.

I lost my job. They said good-bye to my department. That bothered me, but I was tired, too. I was so tired getting four kids up every day, running here and there. The job, the kids were stressing me out. It was like, Okay, I can take a breather and I'll find another job somewhere. But what if I get sick? What's gonna happen? Am I gonna live long enough to see them grow?

I think the worst thing is us being ashamed. Even I'm ashamed. When my daughter's arrest was on TV, people called me. Some didn't have the courage to say it, but I knew what they called me for. They were waiting for me to say something—they hadn't called me in months. I get judged, even at my job. But I guess if Martha Stewart can go to prison, my daughter can, too. That's what I have to keep telling myself. But it doesn't make it any better. I think if I didn't have to worry so much about the financial problem, I could be okay.

They told me, "You might have to give them to the state—put them in the system as abandoned children. You might lose them for 30 days but you can get them back." I won't do it. I said, "It's like 30 *years* for those children." And I don't know if I would get them back. They'd probably separate them. So I'm looking for a job but I'm running out of time.

If I was a mother and these were my kids and I got laid off my job, they would help me get another job or send me to a program and I'd get Medicaid. But I'm just their grandmother and they won't help me.

The children check on me every few minutes—if I'm outa sight, they're gonna check. Especially the baby.

I don't know what to say to them. I don't know whether or not to tell them. The oldest ones saw her on TV, so it's not a secret. And family members and friends tell stuff. They talk about it.

I don't know other children who have a parent in prison. And it's unfair that they don't have playmates and friends. Because all my children are grown, I need to recruit little children because they have none to play with.

I don't know if I'm doing this right. It's so much different now than when I was raising my kids. I'm going to try to make them stay close to home. My main thing is trying to

JACQUELINE FINLEY AND GRANDCHILDREN

get them to understand that they got to be taking care of each other. They are family.

"I have to keep telling them that I'm not the only grandmother raising kids. They need to see that more because they say, 'So and so's mama or dad showed up,' but for them, their granny is the only one coming. The school shouldn't be labeling things 'mama-daughter' things, but instead 'bring your special person.'

"I have one girl that we've been friends since junior high. She comes over. But my other friends are going on trips, and what can I do? One friend says, 'I thought we were going fishing.' And I said, 'Well, the babysitter backed out at the last minute.' We had planned to go to Hot Springs. But I can't do it. I can't just pop up and do things. The majority of my friends at 52 don't have this problem. **JACQUELINE FINLEY**

TEN QUESTIONS OFTEN ASKED BY CHILDREN WHOSE PARENTS ARE IN PRISON

Children need time to adjust to the separation caused by having a parent in prison. But it takes more than time. As we have heard in their voices, children also need to make sense of what has happened to them and to their parent or parents. Because of this, they have many questions.

Some of the questions they ask are straightforward. But sometimes their questions come out indirectly or in their challenging behavior. Incarcerated parents, as well as caregivers of children or other adults in their lives, often have to answer their uncomfortable questions.

Children who are present when a parent is arrested, especially young children, are usually not told where their parents are being taken, when they will be coming home, or why they have to go away. As time goes on, the children have even more questions.

Our childhood experiences shape much of our adult lives. Children who live with these kinds of questions, many of which are not answered to their satisfaction, experience trauma as a result. Frequently that leads to their general mistrust of authority, especially the legal system. Not having their questions answered can also lead children to blame themselves for their parents' absence or to believe that they are destined to follow in their parents' footsteps.

Here are questions that children whose parents are incarcerated often ask, along with suggestions about how to answer them. We will address some of the questions more fully in later sections of the book.

1. WHERE IS MY MOM OR DAD?

Parents and caregivers often believe it is best to protect children by not telling them where their mothers or fathers really are. Children may be told that their parents are working in another state, going to school, or serving in the military. Sometimes children are told that their parents are ill and had to go away for special treatment.

Sooner or later children will realize the truth and know they have been lied to. This tends to hurt their relationship with the persons who have told them the untrue stories and can lead to feelings of distrust that affect their other relationships as well.

While the adult who hides painful reality does so believing it is in the best interests of the child, such an action (or inaction) creates a family secret that results in children feeling ashamed. Most childhood experts advise that children be told the truth.

2. WHEN IS HE OR SHE COMING HOME?

The outcome and schedule of a parent's arrest and/or imprisonment is often uncertain. However, it is important to keep children up-to-date about what parents or caregivers do know. Children need to have concrete information they can deal with, even if it is, "We don't know what will happen yet."

3. WHY IS SHE OR HE IN JAIL OR PRISON?

Sometimes an innocent person is arrested. But when a parent has done wrong, it is important that this wrongdoing is acknowledged. Children need to know that there are consequences when people do things that are against the law or harmful to others.

At the same time, they also need to be reassured that even if someone sometimes does something wrong, it doesn't mean that s/he is necessarily a bad person. A wrongful act does not need to define a person. While a child's parent may be serving the consequences for something wrong s/he did, the parent is still worthy of love and capable of loving.

A child can learn to trust a caregiver who is honest about what a parent has done wrong. This practice of honesty allows the child to believe other things that that caregiver tells her or him as they progress together on this journey.

4. CAN I TALK TO MY MOM OR DAD?

Jails and prisons have specific and often constraining rules about prisoners talking on the phone to their loved ones. Phone calls from prison are often quite expensive and restricted in length. Many times a parent does not have enough money to call home because it is so expensive.

When phone calls are difficult, letters can be especially important. Although young children may find it hard to express themselves through words, they may find it more meaningful to make drawings. As Stacy Bouchet, now an adult, suggests in her reflections on page 52, children often treasure the notes and letters they receive from their parents, as she did from her father.

5. WHEN CAN I SEE MY MOM OR DAD?

It is helpful to explain to children that prisons have specific times for visiting, and that their caretakers will get that information so that they can see their loved ones. If a parent is incarcerated at a distance, the child should be prepared for seeing his or her mother or father infrequently.

Some children are angry and do not want to see their parents, or at least they're ambivalent about the possibility. In general, though, it seems important for children to visit their parents as regularly as possible.

Before the first visit, they should be prepared for the circumstances of the visit. The caregiver should explain the security around the prison. The children should also know that there will be limits upon where they can visit and what they can do with their parents.

Most children want to know what their parent's life is like in prison. They may imagine frightening scenarios. Giving them a sense of the mundane details of everyday life in prison can be helpful. If the child is interested, a caregiver can encourage the parent to describe his or her cell or room and tell what a normal day is like.

6. WHO IS GOING TO TAKE CARE OF ME?

Children in this situation often feel insecure. It is important to let children know who will be caring for them. If there is uncertainty about their living arrangements, children may need to be told that, but they also need to be reassured that plans for their care are being made and that they will not be abandoned. As much as possible, they need stability in their living situations and their relationships.

7. DO MY PARENTS STILL LOVE ME?

When children are separated from their parents, they often worry about whether their parents love and care for them. Most children need assurance that they are loved by their parents no matter where the children happen to be living and with whom. They also value other loving relationships in their lives, but they still want to know about their parents' interest and love.

8. IS THIS MY FAULT?

Children often blame themselves for being separated from their parents or even for their parents' misbehavior. They may imagine that if they had behaved better their parents would still be with them. They need reassurance on three fronts: that what happened to their loved one is not their fault, that it happened because that person did something wrong or harmful, and that this does not mean that their parent is a bad person.

9. WHY DO I FEEL SO SAD AND ANGRY?

Sadness and anger are children's common responses to a parent's incarceration. But most children do not understand their feelings or the origins of them. It is helpful for them to be reassured that their feelings are normal. Ideally, they can be encouraged to talk about their feelings of sadness or anger. If they cannot talk to their immediate caregivers such as their grandparents, they can be invited to talk to school counselors or social workers or even friends. Children often find it helpful to know other children in similar situations because they can understand each other's feelings. Children who find it hard to articulate their feelings can be encouraged to express them through their drawings or other art work.

10. CAN I DO SOMETHING TO HELP?

Children typically feel helpless and responsible. They need to know that their loved ones usually appreciate letters and pictures. They can be encouraged to send them as often as they want to.

*   *   *

These are not the only questions that will come up, of course; they are just some of the most common ones. Remember that these questions have a purpose, even if the child cannot articulate it. He or she is trying to make sense of the situation and to find his or her place in it.

Each family needs to decide how much to say to a child, but all children need to know that they are being told the truth about their parents' incarceration. Depending on their age, they may not need to know, or want to know, all the details. The rule of thumb may be the same as when a young child asks, "Where do babies come from?" The adult does not go into the entire biological facts but simply answers the basic question. Children will generally ask questions as they are ready to hear the information.

We advise that the adult should be as understanding, responsive, and honest as possible, given the circumstances and the child's stage of development.

DEALING WITH EMOTIONS

GRIEF AND LOSS

Children grieve when they are separated from a parent, especially when that separation is forced. The grief they experience often goes unaddressed, and their grief and trauma may be amplified when they don't get answers to their questions.

Parents who are not available because of incarceration cannot provide the comfort their children need. In fact, parents in these circumstances are likely to feel helpless to provide any assistance, given their own circumstances. Family members left behind are often dealing with their own feelings of sadness, anger, and resentment and may not be able to address the children's feelings adequately.

Children naturally carry a mixture of intense feelings as they grieve for parents who are no longer present in their lives—sadness, anger, resentment, confusion, and blame (including self-blame if they don't know the truth). Because of society's stigma associated with incarceration, shame is often a major factor as well. These feelings deepen children's sense of isolation and of being alone. No wonder Nell Bernstein

entitled her book about these children, *All Alone in the World.*

The emotional needs of children of prisoners often go unrecognized in their daily lives because they and their caregivers want to keep the situation a secret in order to maintain some sense of normalcy. Often, however, triggers occur that bring the children's experiences of loss and grief to the surface. Sometimes it happens when they are asked to invite their parents to join them at school or church events. These are often Mother's Day, Father's Day or Christmas events. The celebratory nature of these occasions painfully reminds them of their loss and of how different their lives are from other children.

DEALING WITH SHAME AND STIGMA

Many children in our society are separated from their parents. As we have seen, those who have a parent or parents in prison often experience a greater level of stigma and shame. These feelings are not necessarily triggered by overt expressions from other people. Many times these feelings are self-imposed by children who believe that others cannot understand their lives and so look at them differently than other children. They may interpret their teachers' behavior, for example, as stigmatizing, even when it is not intended that way.

Shame only grows when children do not know the truth about their parents' circumstances and are left to imagine or hear insinuations and misinformation from other children. Understandably, the shame of incarceration is likely a chief reason that caregivers withhold information. Shame, even when it's not directly acknowledged, has a way of being subtly communicated and then assumed by children.

Children may worry that others will find out about their parents' incarceration and make fun of them or isolate them from others in their social group. When children do not know the details of their parents' incarceration and their peers find out and make fun of them, these children, who have now been publicly shamed, find it difficult to distinguish fact from rumor.

Children need help to separate their parents' actions from their own sense of self so they do not internalize the stigma they've experienced. They also need to understand that they are not destined to follow in their parents' footsteps.

Children need to be reassured that they are people of worth, that they are not responsible for their parents' actions, and that they will be able, in time, to be responsible for their own lives. They need opportunities to take pride in their own accomplishments. They can develop more perspective about their circumstances if they are put in touch with other families in similar situations.

DEALING WITH ANGER

Children whose parents are incarcerated often express their grief, loss, shame, and sense of unfairness through anger or defiance. Often their teachers, or other adults they relate to outside their homes, are not aware of the children's situations. These adults often react with disciplinary procedures that can further alienate children at a time when they most need support.

Children's feelings may change daily, often from anger to sadness or depression. When they are angry they may not know who or what they are angry at. They just know that their lives are suddenly very different than they wish, that things seem out of their control, and that they don't have answers to their many questions.

Adults who relate to these children need to understand that children love their parents, even when their parents have committed crimes. The children need to be able to talk about their parents' incarceration to people who are understanding. They need adults who will not condemn their loved ones, who will understand the range of emotions they are experiencing, and who will let them express those emotions so that they can learn appropriate ways of coping.

Children need to know that it is okay to be angry and that those feelings are normal in such an abnormal situation. They often need to talk to someone to be able to sort out their angry feelings. They may be angry at themselves, believing that they are somehow responsible for their parents' arrest. They may be angry at their parents, which compounds their confusion because they also love them and want them back home. They are often angry with the police or courts who took their parents away, often without explanation, as well as with the legal system which is keeping them away.

Anger is a normal response to unexpected and uncontrollable loss, and it usually needs to be expressed and channeled. Anger often needs release. Helping children learn that there are appropriate and inappropriate ways to express anger sometimes requires super-human patience and understanding.

Difficult though it is, caregivers themselves will suffer less if they keep in mind that many factors contribute to children's feelings regarding their parents incarceration. While children's emotions may be directed at their caregivers, often the true objects or sources of their feelings lie elsewhere.

It is also important that caregivers separate their feelings about the situation from the feelings of the children. If caregivers are family members, they may have feelings of resentment or anger about the incarcerated parent. Caregivers need to deal with their own feelings and not seem to be blaming the children. It is helpful if caregivers can understand that children probably have confused feelings about their mother or father being in prison and may not always want to talk with them. Sometimes they may want to, however. Or they may choose to confide in another adult. All of these feelings are normal, and it is important for children's emotional health that they have someone to whom they can voice their feelings, questions, and concerns.

ISOLATION—CHILDREN AND CAREGIVERS NEED SOMEONE TO TALK TO

Because of the stigma and shame that children of incarcerated parents experience, they also endure the isolation that occurs from not being able or willing to tell their stories. Children who are not living with a parent because of divorce, or who lose a parent because of death, are likely to receive care and sympathy from friends, from their teachers, and from others in their lives. Children whose parents are incarcerated find that those necessary supports which provide an outlet for grief are generally not present.

Children need someone who will listen to them without being judgmental so that they do not have to maintain total secrecy. Ideally, they need the safety of talking with others who also have incarcerated parents so that they realize they are not alone in the world with this problem.

STAYING IN TOUCH

As we have seen, it is often important for children to have contact with their parents in prison. How this happens, and how often, may vary with a child's personality or stage of development. Here are some suggestions for staying in touch.

THROUGH PHONE CALLS

Children who hear their parents' voices are reassured that their parents are okay. Depending on the circumstances of the arrest, the first phone call may be the first time the child is reassured that his or her parent is not hurt.

Communication by phone is often difficult inside prisons because calls are expensive and limited. Calls are often abruptly cut off after a certain amount of time has passed without a chance to say good-bye. Knowing that phone calls are limited, parents often feel pressure to say everything at once and to ask a lot of questions. This may put an added strain on their relationships with their children. It is best if parents can simply listen to their children during the phone calls and answer any questions they may have.

BY VISITING

Children need to see their parents and, likewise, parents need to see their children. Being able to maintain relationships with each other is often key to parents' success once they return to the community.

A number of obstacles frequently make visiting loved ones difficult.

- Jails and prisons do not have uniform policies about visiting procedures. Information about these policies isn't always easy to obtain.

- Sometimes the procedures involved with visitation are very intrusive and restrictive. Going through security can be frightening.

- Visiting rooms are often not very welcoming to children. Activities and personal contact are often quite restricted. Local jails usually permit only non-contact visits. A parent and child may be separated by glass and have to talk by phone.

- Loved ones are often placed in prisons that are not geographically close to where children and caregivers live. Caregivers who now must bear the additional financial burden of caring for the children may not be able to afford transportation to visit.

Children may not feel comfortable visiting their parents for a number of reasons. They need the adults in their lives to recognize that they may be confused. Children often feel divided—on the one hand, they really want to see their parents; on the other hand, they may be scared or angry and feel ashamed of those feelings. Additionally, children take their cues from their caregivers. It is best if caregivers do not allow their own anger and irritation to mix into the confusion the children may experience.

Parents in prison frequently have mixed feelings about having their children see them in prison; some, in fact, prefer that their children not see them there. However, it seems that children cope better when they have the opportunity to visit their parents in prison. Furthermore, family connections that have been maintained are a major factor in the successful re-integration of prisoners upon release.

FINDING MOMENTS OF CELEBRATION

Times of celebration, like birthdays and holidays, can be especially difficult when a loved one is in prison. Children often expect these occasions to be wonderful family times. Television shows happy families that are trouble-free with no worries. Children want to be like those happy, carefree families which they see in the movies or read about in books. Children whose parents are in prison soon learn that their lives are otherwise, that these moments can be very painful.

Helping children decide how they want to celebrate special days is important. Do they want to visit their parents for their birthdays, or do they want to stay home with friends that day and visit another day? Perhaps phone calls from their parents would be more beneficial to them on this day.

Making cards or presents as part of a school project for special days, like Mother's or Father's Day, can also be difficult. Again, helping children decide what they need is important. Would they prefer to make their cards for another family member who takes special care of them? Can they make cards for their mothers or fathers, knowing they may not be able to receive the cards in prison but that the cards can be saved for when they see them? Caregivers should make sure that teachers are clued in to the circumstances.

Rather than ignore such times, we encourage caregivers and parents (as much as possible) to be intentional about how to mark them. Perhaps there are other celebrations and rituals during the year that can also help affirm the worth of the children and their parents.

WHEN A PARENT RETURNS

Children often fantasize about what their parents' return will be like. Reality often can't match these expectations.

Ideally, children and their parents who are incarcerated would have had unlimited visits and phone calls. They would be offered all the resources they need, such as therapy and parenting classes to deal with the emotions and challenges they will experience upon the parents' release. Unfortunately, this usually does not happen.

Parents and children often do not know how to relate to each other when they are reunited. Parents may not know how to step into their role. Feeling guilty that they have been absent, they may try to be so present to their children that they seem intrusive to the children. For example, they often try to assume a disciplinary role too quickly. Other parents may be so overwhelmed that they turn away from their responsibilities.

Sometimes a reunion with a parent immediately upon release can be overwhelming for everyone involved. Recently-released parents have plenty of demands placed on them, including the need to locate housing, employment, and transportation. Having also to handle the challenges of parenting can be an additional burden, even though the goal is for parents and children to be reunited.

Several matters need to be taken into account when planning for the reunion. How long has the parent been away from his/her family? How much contact has been maintained with the family? If the parent has been gone for some time, most likely new relationships and attachments have formed in the parent's absence. The children may feel extremely disconnected from their parent. Renewing those bonds will take substantial support and time.

It is important to talk about these issues with children and, if possible, the parents before release. Ideally, parents will have developed a post-release plan addressing their living and work conditions. Specifics about how, where, and when the parents and children will be together can perhaps be included, so that parents are not set up to fail. It is advisable to raise this issue with any professionals or community members who are involved in designing these plans.

A number of models have been developed for families that are facing these kinds of decisions. One model is sometimes called Family Group Decision Making or Family Group Conferences. This approach often involves professionals, but it is always designed to empower families to make decisions and, in some cases, to provide resources for families to carry out their plans.[1] Another model is called Circle Processes. A Circle Process is a specific way for family members (and others with primary interest) to come together to safely and respectfully explore issues and make decisions.[2] (More information about these approaches may be found in *Suggested Resources*, page 92.)

Caregivers, whether another parent or other family members, may have mixed feelings about the return of the parent who has been incarcerated. While caregivers may be excited and possibly relieved to turn over or share the responsibility, they may also be worried about the ability of the returning parent to provide adequately for the children. Suddenly losing the primary care of a child to a parent who has been absent might be worrisome and also create a sense of loss for those providing care. Despite conflicting emotions, caregivers ultimately want to know that the children they have lovingly cared for are emotionally and physically safe.

Reentry can be tricky for all involved and often requires resources beyond the family. But a successful reentry is important for everyone involved.

SELF-CARE FOR FAMILY CAREGIVERS

Caring for children has its challenges. Caring for children who are not one's own, who are dealing with traumatic experiences of separation and loss, can be doubly challenging. The following are a few suggestions for family members or foster parents who are caring for these children.

"WHAT'S MY STUFF?"

Those of us in helping professions need to continually ask ourselves, What's my stuff? When am I projecting my own feelings and needs onto the other person? And when the other person is directing feelings toward me, to what extent are those feelings really about me? When a child or young person is acting out, is the caregiver really the object of that youngster's anger? Or is the source and object of that anger elsewhere? In the case of children separated from their parents by prison, the latter is often true.

GETTING A BREAK

Caregivers need a break from providing care for extra members in their households. This is especially true when the responsibility is full-time. As Jacqueline Finley says earlier in this book (page 58), grandparents who are caregivers often don't have the energy that a younger caregiver would have. Moreover, times have changed, and the culture of today's young people is different than it was when they raised their own children. Older caregivers often find themselves bewildered by the rules and expectations of youth culture.

Caregivers need breaks for their emotional and physical well-being. In fact, they deserve them and shouldn't feel guilty about asking friends and family members to step in occasionally.

DEALING WITH THEIR OWN SENSE OF LOSS AND SHAME

Often when persons assume the care of others' children, their expectations and plans for their own lives suddenly are put on hold. This is especially true for grandparents. Carolyn and Darnell Hobbs' experience (page 54) is common. They had expected their "golden years" to be a time of freedom and relaxation after raising a family and being busy with their careers. Now friends their own age are traveling and involved in recreation; they often don't understand why Carolyn and Darnell aren't available.

Even though these persons love the children in their care and are glad to be making a difference in their lives, it is normal that they would struggle with a sense of loss and unfairness. It is important that they recognize and accept these feelings for what they are.

Like the children, these caregiving family members of the incarcerated may also struggle with a sense of shame about what their loved ones have done or about the lives they are leading. These relatives need to know that they are certainly not alone in their shame. Nor are they responsible for the choices their loved ones have made. In fact, it takes strength and courage to give care to the children of their relatives who are in prison.

These family members also need to find a safe place to talk through their feelings—with friends or counselors—and we encourage caregivers to seek out listeners they can trust.

GETTING FINANCIAL AND OTHER ASSISTANCE

States vary with the amount of financial assistance they make available. Policies are often inequitable. For example, family caregivers may not receive the same financial support as foster-care providers. In fact, family caregivers may not receive any financial support. Some states require that children become their wards before they make assistance available. But if families permit their children to become wards of the state, they fear that they may forfeit eventually caring for the children.

In some states, child welfare agencies can help families caring for children of incarcerated parents by referring them to community-based agencies without conducting a formal investigation. When this is possible, it avoids risks of sanction and separation that a formal investigation could trigger.

We encourage direct caregivers to check with public and private social service providers to find out what resources are available in their communities.

SUGGESTIONS FOR THIRD-PARTY CAREGIVERS

FOR SCHOOLS

School systems play a huge role in the lives of children. Teachers, social workers, and guidance counselors can provide invaluable stability and support in what is otherwise an often chaotic and unpredictable existence. A number of the young people interviewed for this project noted the important role that one or more teachers had in their lives.

But some children tell stories of hurt from school. Schools are not necessarily prepared for, nor are they always aware of, those children who have an incarcerated parent. Some families, or the children themselves, may make the decision not to tell the school, given the social stigmas associated with parental incarceration.

Collaboration between the child welfare and the educational systems would be a critical first step in setting up supports for children who have an incarcerated parent. The child-welfare worker can assist by sorting out what the child needs from the educational system. The caseworker can then act as a liaison between the child and the

school to identify those supports that the school can provide. The caseworker can also help the child decide which teacher or staff member to confide in. In their article, "Children of Incarcerated Parents and the School System," Emani G. Davis and Dee Ann Newell recommend to schools what they can do to support children within the system who have an incarcerated parent.[3]

1. For younger children, include storybooks in the classroom that describe a visit to a parent who is incarcerated. There are several excellent books that seek to minimize the stigma for the child.[4] (See http://fcnetwork.org for suggestions.)

2. Be aware of the rigid prison visiting requirements and hours, and understand that children may miss class or extra-curricular activities when visiting their incarcerated parents.

   Some schools now accept pre-scheduled collect calls from parents in prison, allowing them to speak with their children and with their children's teachers. This opportunity should be explored whenever possible.

3. Try to engage incarcerated parents by including them in conference calls about their children's work and progress. Send them their children's schoolwork and report cards and the school's newsletters. If there is a storybook program in the prison that provides a taping of the parent reading aloud for the child, permit the taping to be used in the child's classroom, but without identifying the parent as imprisoned.

4. Work with experts in your area to develop trainings for all school personnel around the issues of children with incarcerated parents.

FOR MENTORS

Mentors can be an important presence in the lives of young people whose parents are in prison. This is especially true since full-time caregivers are often overwhelmed by the added stress created by caring for these children.

Mentors can provide objective listening ears and support as children struggle with their parents' incarceration. They can also assist in determining resources within the community that would support both children and caregivers during this stressful period of their lives as they seek to adjust to a new reality.

Mentors, like other caregivers, need to remember that when children act out, they're likely not focused primarily on undoing them as mentors. Children are probably looking for attention or testing whether the mentors will stick with them. As Stacey Bouchet says in her interview (page 52), it is important that mentors hang in for the long haul—at least a year—and not give up when children act out.

Many communities offer programs for mentoring young people. Big Brothers/Big Sisters is one such organization that can be a resource for mentors or a place to volunteer as a mentor.

"IT MAKES YOU STRONGER"

The issues these children face come through clearly in their words. But what is also obvious is their strength and resilience. In spite of their challenges, these children are often hopeful, full of energy, and remarkably capable. They need security and support, yet they often develop an amazing inner strength. As Taylor says, "You have to grow up fast."

Jermaine has developed into a reflective and gifted young adult. Brittany and Taylor have learned that although their parents have made mistakes, they as children are not necessarily bad, nor do their parents not love them. Sasha's father has come to personalize her conscience. By participating in a play about children of prisoners, Taylor has learned that she has dramatic skills that she didn't know she had. Anabel found her voice through art.

Stacey, in her late 30s, is in a position to look back and reflect on the impact of her father's incarceration on her childhood. Clearly, the experience presented her with serious challenges, but she also learned a great deal. Today she has a Ph.D. and works with programming for children at risk. Her experience motivates her and allows her to identify with these children.

We have highlighted some of the problems and difficulties faced by children whose parents are in prison. But we believe firmly that it is essential to emphasize and encourage their competencies. Every child has worth. Each child has gifts. Each has contributions to make.

To young people who have the misfortune of having a parent, or both parents, in prison, yes, it feels unfair. You do not deserve this. But you are not alone. You do not have to let this situation define who you are. As Taylor says, "I want other kids to know that even though your parents are locked up, they're not bad people.

"And I want them to know that we'll get through it. As long as we have someone there to help us, we can get through it. It makes you stronger."

Part III

A Matter of Justice

I was serving time with a woman who had only 10 years to do. Twenty years later, some kid comes up to me and says, "Aren't you Ms. Mechie? My mom told me to look you up when I got here." At first I was glad to see someone else's child, like they dropped by my house to visit. Then it occurred to me just how tragic a scene this is. Now it happens all the time—I'm forever looking out for somebody's kid here in prison.

I see three generations of mothers, all in prison at once. For those who lack clear evidence of intergenerational incarceration—here we all are!

MARIE SCOTT

Life-sentenced Marie Scott has made her concern about the revolving door of prison families her lifework, to the extent that she is able to from behind bars.

For some of the reasons we have seen earlier, when a parent is incarcerated, the children who are involved are likely to suffer from anxiety, attention disorder, traumatic stress, and even post-traumatic stress disorder (PTSD).[5] Many feel victimized by forces beyond their control. Many grow up feeling that life is unfair.

Research suggests that children of prisoners are five times more likely to go to prison themselves than other children.[6] In fact, as many as half of the boys in this situation may wind up behind bars.[7] This is a frightening reality, destined to further fuel the prison expansion of the last decades. It also frequently becomes a self-fulfilling prophecy because many children who have a parent in prison develop a fatalism about their own futures. As a result, their sense of personal power over their own lives may be reduced.

The trauma resulting from parental incarceration may help to explain the offending behavior of some children. Carolyn Yoder, in *The Little Book of Trauma Healing*, describes common responses in the cycle of trauma and victimization and how, when unhealed,

MARIE ("MECHIE") SCOTT & DAUGHTER HOPE IN 1993

Marie's parents were in prison, and she is serving a life sentence herself. Her son served time in prison. After he was released he established a successful home repair business, but recently he was killed in a motorcycle accident.

this trauma cycle can become a victim/perpetrator cycle.[8] In other words, when people who feel victimized cannot find a way to heal, they can themselves become perpetrators.

To put it another way, much aggression is a response to unaddressed trauma. Psychiatrist Sandra Bloom says that unresolved trauma tends to be reenacted.[9] It is reenacted in the lives of those who have been traumatized, but also in the lives of their families, and even in future generations.

The trauma associated with parental incarceration may fuel a cycle of offending, resulting in the intergenerational incarceration that concerns lifer Marie Scott.

> "The dissolution of families, the harm to children—and the resultant perpetuation of the cycle of crime and incarceration from one generation to the next—may be the most profound and damaging effect of our current penal structure."
>
> —Nell Bernstein, *All Alone in the World*

Some communities have programs, often based in nonprofit organizations, to work with these families. Arkansas is fortunate to have Arkansas Voices for the Children Left Behind, an exemplary service and advocacy program that was one of the collaborators with us on this project. (For more information on this and other programs see *Suggested Resources* on page 92.) But such programs are all too scarce in many communities, and the downturn in the economy during the past years has hit them hard.

The Bill of Rights for Children of the Incarcerated, initially written by Nell Bernstein, is becoming an important rallying point for raising awareness and developing policies to address these children's needs. It goes beyond the incarceration experience itself, encouraging police departments to develop more child-sensitive policies when parents are being arrested.

CHILDREN OF INCARCERATED PARENTS:
A BILL OF RIGHTS

1. I have the right to be kept safe and informed at the time of my parent's arrest.

2. I have the right to be heard when decisions are made about me.

3. I have the right to be considered when decisions are made about my parent.

4. I have the right to be well cared for in my parent's absence.

5. I have the right to speak with, see, and touch my parent.

6. I have the right to support as I face my parent's incarceration.

7. I have the right not to be judged, blamed, or labeled because my parent is incarcerated.

8. I have the right to a lifelong relationship with my parent.

—San Francisco Children of Incarcerated Parents
www.sfcipp.org/right1.html

A MATTER OF JUSTICE

Children's rights represent an important step forward within the rights-based framework of the criminal justice system. But the situation of these children raises more basic questions about our approach to justice overall.

Should we be relying so heavily on prisons as a response to wrongdoing? The United States has, after all, the highest rate of incarceration in the world, yet imprisonment has no demonstrable effect on crime rates. According to a 2008 report by the Pew's Center on the States, one in 100 adults in the U.S. is now in prison.

The weight of this pattern of imprisonment does not fall equally on all Americans. The majority of the children included in this project are children of color. While these proportions may not exactly parallel the proportions in the prison system as a whole, they emphasize a disturbing reality: our prison population is made up of a much higher proportion of people of color than their numbers in the population or their patterns of offending would suggest. The Pew report found that one in nine young African American men between ages 20 and 34 is now behind bars. In some cities, one in four, or even one in three, young African Americans are held within the control of the criminal justice system on any given day. For many, the experience of prison has become a rite of passage into manhood.

All of this raises larger questions that go beyond our country's prison policy. It raises questions about our society's entire approach to justice. Should we be so preoccupied with punishment? Should we not be giving more attention than we do to the needs of crime victims? What about treating and rehabilitating offenders in order to prevent further offending? What shall we do to support the families of both victims and offenders who are impacted by crime, yet so often neglected? Should we be so intent on making sure offenders get what they "deserve" while neglecting their responsibilities to the people and communities they have harmed?

To put it in simplistic terms, our criminal justice approach tends to be driven by three questions:

1. What laws were broken?
2. Who did it?
3. What do they "deserve"? What they deserve, we usually assume, is punishment, often prison.

If these questions guide our search for justice, is it any wonder that victims are neglected? Or that imprisonment rates are so high? Or that so little attention is given to the families of those who are incarcerated? It comes down to what we want of justice.

A NEEDS APPROACH TO JUSTICE

Restorative justice is a philosophy and a practice of justice that has emerged in many communities throughout the world over the past several decades. It offers an alternative approach to justice—one that focuses more on needs and responsibilities and less on "deserts" and punishment.[10]

A primary goal of justice in this view is to acknowledge and repair harm—the harm *caused* by wrongdoing, but also the harm *revealed* by wrongdoing. What often matters most about crime is the harm that is caused—harm to people, harm to relationships. But wrongdoing is often a symptom that something is wrong in the life of the offending one as well.

Restorative justice is built upon three assumptions:

1. Wrongdoing is fundamentally a violation of people and interpersonal relationships. It is about harm, and harm creates needs.
2. Violations create obligations or responsibilities. The central obligation is to put right the wrongs to the extent possible.
3. Those who have been impacted by, or otherwise have a stake in, the situation should be involved in the solution as much as possible.

Restorative justice realizes that three sets of stakeholders are involved: victims and their families; offenders and their families; and the larger community that is impacted and also has responsibilities for its members.

In its simplest form, restorative justice principles can be stated like this: A just approach to wrong requires that we...

1. acknowledge and repair the harm that has been done,
2. take appropriate responsibility to repair this harm and address the resulting needs,
3. engage all who have a stake in the situation to address the needs of all involved.

If we were to take a restorative approach to justice, we would begin with three different questions than those that guide the criminal justice approach:

1. Who has been hurt by this action?
2. What are their needs?
3. Whose obligation is it to address these harms and needs?

We would also go on to ask several additional questions. What caused this? Who has a stake in or has been impacted by this? How can they be involved in sorting out the obligations and addressing the harms and causes?

Since crime is essentially about harm, restorative justice has rightfully emphasized the attention that the direct victims of crime should receive. Those who offend should be encouraged to understand that harm and to take steps to repair that harm as much as possible. Ideally, the needs that have motivated offenders to do harm would also be addressed in order to reduce re-offending.

But true justice would also address what Elizabeth Beck and her colleagues call the "collateral damage" of crime: the harm to families of victims and families of offenders.[11] In many ways, in fact, families of offenders are themselves victims of their family member's behavior and the consequences that befall the offenders. All too often, offenders' families are also victims of the justice process.

Like crime victims, families of those in prison have needs resulting from (and sometimes revealed by) the harm. A truly just approach would seek to address their needs and involve them in doing so.

As we have seen, families of prisoners have many basic social service and financial needs. Support for these families would go far toward creating a healthier society and could help to reduce future offending. But like crime victims, these families often have some specific "justice needs" as well—needs that can and should be addressed in a justice process.

JUSTICE NEEDS OF FAMILIES

We have said that victims of crime have a cluster of needs that can be best addressed by a restorative justice process.[12] When these justice needs are addressed, victims may be assisted in moving on in their journeys to transcend the harm. When victims get stuck on their journeys, it may be because their justice needs are not met. While we do not wish to over-emphasize the parallels, we are struck by some similarities between the needs of victims and the needs of families of prisoners.

Like victims, these families need information and answers to the questions that arise from the wrongdoing, as well as information about what is going on in the justice process. What happened? Why did it happen? What is happening in the justice process? Answers to such questions help people to restore their sense of meaning and safety. The lack of answers can be stressful and even traumatic. In these pages we have heard children asking these kinds of questions.

Like victims, families may need to tell

their stories and to have them affirmed. It is through telling their stories that human beings put words to the harm they've experienced. It is by telling stories that any one of us incorporates hard things into our stories and lives, giving meaning to them. It is by having our individual stories heard that our realities are affirmed. Support groups for these families can be one way that this particular need can be met. The two of us have tried in a small way to provide an opportunity for families to tell a part of their stories in this project.

Families of those who are incarcerated, like victims, often need to experience being involved or empowered. When their loved one has done wrong, when he or she is taken from their lives, families often feel disempowered. When they have so little recognition and so little voice in the justice and punishment process, they are further disempowered. Opportunities to be involved and heard can assist them in their journeys of healing.

Another need which victims often express is their wish to be validated and vindicated. This need seems to have a number of dimensions. It usually involves the desire for a moral statement about who is responsible for what. It may involve removing the shame and humiliation they feel. It often requires a "setting right" by having the offender acknowledge the wrongdoing and then undertaking an effort to make things right through apology and restitution.

Families of offenders may have somewhat similar needs as those of victims. They may wish for their family member to understand and acknowledge the harm s/he has done to the family itself and to take responsibility for it. They, too, may need to find a way to rid themselves of the shame and humiliation they experience.

The needs-orientation of restorative justice may provide a way to hear and begin to make right some of the needs of families who are the direct or indirect victims of their family member's behavior.

Restorative justice also emphasizes obligations: the obligations offenders have to do something about the harm they have caused, but the obligations of others as well. Using a grid of restorative justice, rather than punishment only, would help those who are in prison to understand the harm they may have done to their family members and to accept responsibility for it. A just response would help our communities to care for those among us who are hurt and vulnerable. That certainly includes children of the incarcerated. These children have done nothing to deserve the plight they are in. For our own security, if for nothing else, it is in our interest to care for these children.

THREE VALUES

Ultimately, restorative justice is about the values that guide our lives. Three values are especially important. We might be call these the three "R's" of restorative justice: respect, responsibility, and relationships.

We are convinced that much offending arises out of issues of respect and disrespect. Aggression is often a way to obtain respect, though in unfortunate ways. Similarly, our justice system often fails to prevent crime: just as violence begets violence, disrespect begets disrespect. As we have listened to victims, we have found that disrespect is part of their trauma—disrespect by the offender, sometimes by the system, sometimes even by their loved ones. Those closest to the victims frequently can't tolerate or understand their anger or emotions, and they may subtly blame them for what happened or urge them to forgive the offender prematurely.

Families of those in prison also grapple with issues of respect and disrespect. They sometimes feel like their loved ones' behavior shows disrespect for them and their values. And they often feel disrespected by the legal and prison systems and by society at large. *Restorative justice is essentially about respecting all parties, including the families of those who have done wrong.*

Restorative justice also encourages responsibility, the second "R": responsibility on the part of those who cause harm, but also the responsibility of all of us for one another.

That leads to what is probably the most central value, the third "R" of restorative justice: relationships. In a culture that puts so much emphasis on individual rights and personal autonomy, restorative justice reminds us of what most of our cultural and religious traditions emphasize: we are interconnected. Our behavior affects other people, and we are responsible for the consequences. Whether we like it or not, we are in this world together. The harm of one is the harm of all, and the good of one is the good of all.

*   *   *

Our relationships with others—our family, our friends, our colleagues, victims, offenders, and our community—can be described by using the metaphor of a web. Like a web, we are interconnected in various ways. When that web is broken, our relationships and communities become weakened. Many see restorative justice as a way to reconnect those broken strands.

Like a web, we are all interconnected. The children in these pages are in some sense our children. What happens to them affects all of us.

APPENDIX A
BILL OF RIGHTS FOR CHILDREN OF THE INCARCERATED AND SOME POLICY IMPLICATIONS

The San Francisco Children of Incarcerated Parents Partnership has proposed the following steps toward making the Bill of Rights for Children of Incarcerated Parents a reality. (See http://www.sfcipp.org/rights.html)

1. I have the right to be kept safe and informed at the time of my parent's arrest.
- Develop arrest protocols that support and protect children.
- Offer children and/or their caregivers basic information about the post-arrest process.

2. I have the right to be heard when decisions are made about me.
- Train staff at institutions whose constituency includes children of incarcerated parents to recognize and address these children's needs and concerns.
- Tell the truth.
- Listen.

3. I have the right to be considered when decisions are made about my parent.
- Review current sentencing law in terms of its impact on children and families.
- Turn arrest into an opportunity for family preservation.
- Include a family impact statement in pre-sentence investigation reports.

4. I have the right to be well cared for in my parent's absence.
- Support children by supporting their caretakers.
- Offer subsidized guardianship.

5. I have the right to speak with, see and touch my parent.
- Provide access to visiting rooms that are child-centered, non-intimidating and conducive to bonding.
- Consider proximity to family when siting prisons and assigning prisoners.
- Encourage child welfare departments to facilitate contact.

6. I have the right to support as I face my parent's incarceration.
- Train adults who work with young people to recognize the needs and concerns of children whose parents are incarcerated.
- Provide access to specially trained therapists, counselors, and/or mentors.
- Save five percent for families.

7. I have the right not to be judged, blamed or labeled because my parent is incarcerated.
- Create opportunities for children of incarcerated parents to communicate with and support each other.
- Create a truth fit to tell.
- Consider differential response when a parent is arrested.

8. I have the right to a lifelong relationship with my parent.
- Re-examine the Adoption and Safe Families Act.
- Designate a family services coordinator at prisons and jails.
- Support incarcerated parents upon reentry.
- Focus on rehabilitation and alternatives to incarceration.

APPENDIX B

A Set of Core Principles when seeking policy initiatives for children of incarcerated parents was developed by the Open Society Institute partners during the 2006–2008 OSI Senior Justice Fellowship project of Dee Ann Newell. These include the following:[13]

1. This policy work is quite urgent. Too many children are hurting, and their numbers are growing. We must act NOW.

2. Our work should not further diminish or stigmatize these children. Our efforts should focus on their amazing strengths and resiliencies, while we seek to mitigate the traumas they are exposed to and support their healing from past traumas.

3. Our focus on the children must include policies and services that include their families and their incarcerated parents. For example, a parent suffering from addiction must have accessible and substantive drug treatment in order for the parent-child relationship to become healthy. Children must be permitted to visit their parents in supportive conditions conducive to maintaining the parent-child relationship.

4. These eight rights are rights that every child deserves, whether they affect only one child or three million children, whether children of the incarcerated or all children left behind for all the reasons this might occur. These rights are rights for all children, for the children's sake and not because of other beneficial consequences.

5. The children are the true experts and must be given opportunities to speak with comfort and safety and to be carefully listened to by advocates and policymakers.

SUGGESTED RESOURCES

ORGANIZATIONS & WEBSITES

Family & Corrections Network: The National Resource Center on Children and Families of the Incarcerated (www.fcnetwork.org). This national network of organizations provides a rich variety of resources. See for example the *Children of Prisoners Library*: Different Children / Different Behaviors by Ann Adalist-Estrin, #304 and Questions from Caregivers, #202.

National Community Service Resource Center (www.nationalserviceresources .org/service-activities/mentoring-children-of-prisoners). Provides information on mentoring children of prisoners.

San Francisco Children of Incarcerated Parents Partnership (www.sfcipp.org). Provides leadership on the Bill of Rights for Children of Incarcerated Parents policy and practice models and issues, including legislative initiatives.

www.restorativejustice.org. Excellent source of information on restorative justice, including links to other websites.

Suggestion: Numerous specific programs and resources may be found by searching the Internet using phrases such as children of prisoners, families of prisoners, children of the incarcerated, etc.

PUBLICATIONS

Bernstein, Nell. *All Alone in the World: Children of the Incarcerated.* The New Press, New York, 2007.

Beck, Elizabeth, Sarah Britto and Arlene Andrews. *In the Shadow of Death: Restorative Justice and Death Row Families.* Oxford University Press, New York, NY, 2007.

Bouchet, Stacey M. *Children and Families with Incarcerated Parents: Exploring Development in the Field and Opportunities for Growth.* The Annie E. Casey Foundation, Baltimore, MD, 2008. (See www.aecf.org/KnowledgeCenter/ Publications.aspx?pubguid= {E1181F44-1C8E-4E44-85EA-1C7870CD2B68})

Davies, Elizabeth, Diana Brazzell, Nancy G. La Vigne, and Tracey L. Sollenberger. *Understanding the Needs and Experiences of Children of Incarcerated Parents: Views from Mentors.* Urban Institute, Justice Policy Center. February, 2008. (See www.urban.org/url.cfm?ID= 411615)

MacRae, Allan and Howard Zehr. *The Little Book of Family Group Conferences: New Zealand Style.* Good Books, Intercourse, PA, 2004.

Pranis, Kay. *The Little Book of Circle Processes: A New/Old Approach to Peacemaking.* Good Books, Intercourse, PA, 2005.

Thursday's Child: Broken Bonds: Understanding and Addressing the Needs of Children with Incarcerated Mothers. Urban Institute, Justice Policy Center, February, 2008. (See www.urban.org/url.cfm?ID= 500052)

Walker, Claire A. *Children of Incarcerated Parents.* Pittsburgh Child Guidance Foundation, March, 2005. (See www.foundationcenter.org/ grantmaker/childguidance/ linked_files/incarcerated.pdf)

Zehr, Howard. *The Little Book of Restorative Justice.* Good Books, Intercourse, PA, 2002.

Zehr, Howard. *Doing Life: Reflections of Men and Women Serving Life Sentences.* Good Books, Intercourse, PA, 1996.

AUDIOVISUAL RESOURCES

When a Parent is in Prison. Exhibit available on loan from the Mennonite Central Committee Resource Library (us.mcc.org/ programs/peacebuilding/ resources/exhibits).

Shadows: Children, Families and the Legacy of Incarceration. Drama produced by TOVA: Artistic Project for Social Change. DVD version available from Family & Corrections Network (www.fcnetwork.org/products-publications/nrccfi/books-films).

ENDNOTES

[1] See, for example, Allan MacRae and Howard Zehr, *The Little Book of Family Group Conferences, New Zealand Style* (Intercourse, PA: Good Books, 2004). American Humane (www.americanhumane.org) and the International Institute for Restorative Practices (www.iirp.org) provide information on family group processes.

[2] See Kay Pranis, *The Little Book of Circle Processes* (Intercourse, PA: Good Books, 2005).

[3] "CW 360°: Children of Incarcerated Parents," University of Minnesota Center for Advanced Studies in Child Welfare, Spring, 2008, 20. (www.f2f.ca.gov/res/pdf/cw360.pdf).

[4] See www.fcnetwork.org for suggestions.

[5] Nell Bernstein, *All Alone in the World: Children of the Incarcerated* (New York: The New Press, 2007), p. 3. Elizabeth Beck, Sarah Britto and Arlene Andrews, *In the Shadow of Death: Restorative Justice and Death Row Families* (New York: Oxford University Press, 2007), p. 97.

[6] Beck et al, 95.

[7] Bernstein, 3.

[8] Carolyn Yoder, *The Little Book of Trauma Healing: When Violence Strikes and Community Security Is Threatened* (Intercourse, PA: Good Books, 2005).

[9] Sandra Bloom, *Creating Sanctuary: Toward the Evolution of Sane Societies* (New York, NY: Routledge, 1997).

[10] See Howard Zehr, *The Little Book of Restorative Justice* (Intercourse, PA: Good Books, 2002).

[11] Beck, et al.

[12] For a fuller description see Howard Zehr, *Transcending: Reflections of Crime Victims* (Intercourse, PA: Good Books, 2001).

[13] Dee Ann Newell, "The OSI Bill of Rights Technical Assistance Project for Children of Incarcerated Parents," *Women, Girls and Criminal Justice* (Kingston, NJ: Civic Research Institute, 2008).

ABOUT THE AUTHORS AND PHOTOGRAPHER

Howard Zehr is widely known as "the grandfather of restorative justice." Since 1996 he has been Professor of Restorative Justice at the Center for Justice & Peacebuilding at Eastern Mennonite University, Harrisonburg, VA, an international graduate program for justice and peacebuilding practitioners.

Howard has published several other portrait/interview books including *Doing Life: Reflections of Men and Women Serving Life Sentences* and *Transcending: Reflections of Crime Victims* (both with Good Books). He has authored numerous other books and publications; best known are *The Little Book of Restorative Justice* (Good Books) and *Changing Lenses: A New Focus for Crime and Justice*.

He is a frequent speaker and consultant on justice issues in North America and internationally. Zehr has also worked professionally as a photographer.

Lorraine Stutzman Amstutz is Co-Director of Mennonite Central Committee's Office on Justice and Peacebuilding. She provides consulting and training for agencies and communities seeking to implement programs of restorative justice.

Lorraine has written numerous articles, co-authored *The Little Book of Restorative Discipline for Schools* (with Judy H. Mullet), and written *The Little Book of Victim Offender Conferencing: Bringing Victims and Offenders Together in Dialogue* (both published by Good Books).

She has served on the international Victim Offender Mediation Association (VOMA) Board.

Group Discounts for *What Will Happen to Me?*

If you would like to inquire about ordering multiple copies of **What Will Happen to Me?** by Howard Zehr and Lorraine Stutzman Amstutz, for groups you know or are a part of, please contact Good Books at 1/800-762-7171, Ext. 221 between 9:00 a.m. and 5:00 p.m. ET.
